The 3 MINUTE 90 DAY Gratitude Journal For Girls

The Life Graduate Publishing Group

No part of this book may be scanned, reproduced or distributed in any printed or electronic form without the prior permission of the author or publisher.

Copyright - The Life Graduate Publishing Group 2021 - All Rights Reserved

Stronger Friendships

Kindness and Appreciation

The benefits of
 GRATITUDE

Better Health

Increased Energy

Greater Sleep Quality

Starting Your Day With Gratitude

Congratulations on starting your very own Gratitude Journal. By completing your journal each day, it will help you to appreciate all of the wonderful things around you!

This journal has been created in a clear, fun and interactive one page format to make it nice and easy for you to write down how you feel, the things you enjoyed during the day and includes spaces for drawings and to include photos if you choose.

The journal asks you to write down 2 or 3 things each day that you're grateful for. These may be things that have happened during the day, during the week or something happening in your life right now? To help you, it could be things that you do with family and friends like vacations, the accomplishments you have earned for school, sports events or activities, new friendships you have formed or anything else that you are grateful for.

Just sparing 3 minutes each day to think about the things in life that matter to you will boost your confidence and energy levels and you will take new leaps and bounds every day.

Gratitude and mindfulness activities like journaling are so important, and we all need to think about what we are grateful for every day.

Remember, the best attitude to have is gratitude!

How to use your journal

Step 1.
Complete your journal somewhere that is nice and peaceful for you.

Step 2.
Follow the prompts on each page. Start by writing down the day and date and then move onto the first question.

Step 3.
Write down exactly how you feel. Being honest with ourselves is an important start on our gratitude journey.

Step 4.
Once completed, place in a safe place and in a location that will remind you to complete the journal tomorrow. To help, it is sometimes good to set a daily alarm for the same time each day.

MY 3 MINUTE GRATITUDE JOURNAL

DAY: MON TUES WED THU FRI SAT SUN

1. I helped this person today..
   ....

2. Write below what you did to be kind.....

{   }

3. Gratitude. These are 3 things I am grateful for...

1 _____
2 _____
3 _____

4. I would rate today....
Color in your 'STAR' rating for today.
1 star = I didn't have a good day
5 stars = EXCELLENT!

★ ★ ★ ★ ★

MY 3 MINUTE GRATITUDE JOURNAL

DAY: MON TUES WED THU FRI SAT SUN

1. Circle where you felt on the 'happiness' scale today?

2. These are 3 things I am grateful for...

1 _____

2 _____

3 _____

3. What did you enjoy most about today?.......

4. Who did you say 'thank you' to today?

MY 3 MINUTE GRATITUDE JOURNAL

DAY: MON TUES WED THU FRI SAT SUN

1. My Happiness Rating
Circle how you feel?

- Happy
- Just OK
- I feel a little sad today

2. I would like to say thank you for...

1 _____
2 _____
3 _____

3. This person was kind today.

4. What did you enjoy most about today?.......

_____

MY 3 MINUTE GRATITUDE JOURNAL

DAY: MON TUES WED THU FRI SAT SUN

1. Gratitude
These are 2 things that really make me happy!

1. _____
2. _____

2. I felt happiest today when...

Write below what you did to be kind today?

_____
_____
_____

3. How I was feeling today...
Draw your face here.

MY 3 MINUTE GRATITUDE JOURNAL

DAY: MON TUES WED THU FRI SAT SUN

1. Gratitude

These are 2 things that really make me happy!

1 _____
2 _____

2. Today is about expressing how you feel.

Draw or sketch anything you want below.

MY 3 MINUTE GRATITUDE JOURNAL

DAY: MON TUES WED THU FRI SAT SUN

1. I helped this person today...
ooooooooooooooooooooooooooooooooooooooooooooooooooooo

2. Write below what you did to be kind......

{

}

3. Gratitude. These are 3 things I am grateful for...

1 _____
2 _____
3 _____

4. I would rate today....
Color in your 'STAR' rating for today.
1 star = I didn't have a good day
5 stars = EXCELLENT!

☆ ☆ ☆ ☆ ☆

MY 3 MINUTE GRATITUDE JOURNAL

DAY: MON TUES WED THU FRI SAT SUN

1. Circle where you felt on the 'happiness' scale today?

2. These are 3 things I am grateful for...
   1 _____
   2 _____
   3 _____

3. What did you enjoy most about today?.......

4. Who did you say 'thank you' to today?

MY 3 MINUTE GRATITUDE JOURNAL

DAY: MON TUES WED THU FRI SAT SUN

1. My Happiness Rating
Circle how you feel?

- Happy
- Just OK
- I feel a little sad today

2. I would like to say thank you for...

1 _____
2 _____
3 _____

3. This person was kind today.

4. What did you enjoy most about today?.......

_____

MY 3 MINUTE GRATITUDE JOURNAL

DAY: MON TUES WED THU FRI SAT SUN

1. Gratitude

These are 2 things that really make me happy!

1. _____
2. _____

2. I felt happiest today when...

Write below what you did to be kind today?

_____
_____
_____

3. How I was feeling today...
   Draw your face here.

MY 3 MINUTE GRATITUDE JOURNAL

DAY: MON TUES WED THU FRI SAT SUN

1. I helped this person today.. ....

2. Write below what you did to be kind......

{   }

3. Gratitude. These are 3 things I am grateful for...

1 _____
2 _____
3 _____

4. I would rate today....
Color in your 'STAR' rating for today.
1 star = I didn't have a good day
5 stars = EXCELLENT!

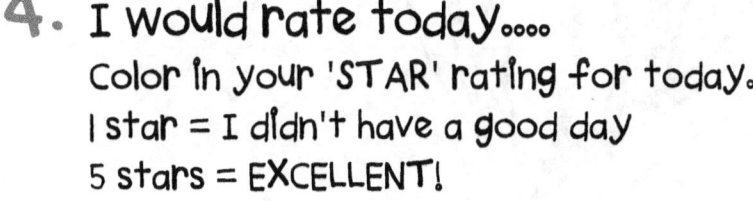

Color in the flower and relax today.

MEMORIES AND HAPPY MOMENTS

Do you have a photo that you would like to include here?

MY 3 MINUTE GRATITUDE JOURNAL

DAY: MON TUES WED THU FRI SAT SUN

1. I helped this person today.. ○○

2. Write below what you did to be kind.....

{   }

3. Gratitude. These are 3 things I am grateful for...

1 _____
2 _____
3 _____

4. I would rate today....
Color in your 'STAR' rating for today.
1 star = I didn't have a good day
5 stars = EXCELLENT!

★ ★ ★ ★ ★

MY 3 MINUTE GRATITUDE JOURNAL

DAY: MON TUES WED THU FRI SAT SUN

1. Circle where you felt on the 'happiness' scale today?

2. These are 3 things I am grateful for...

1. _____

2. _____

3. _____

3. What did you enjoy most about today?.......

4. Who did you say 'thank you' to today?

MY 3 MINUTE GRATITUDE JOURNAL

DAY: MON TUES WED THU FRI SAT SUN

1. My Happiness Rating
Circle how you feel?

- Happy
- Just OK
- I feel a little sad today

2. I would like to say thank you for...

1 _____
2 _____
3 _____

3. This person was kind today.

4. What did you enjoy most about today?......

_____

MY 3 MINUTE GRATITUDE JOURNAL

DAY: MON TUES WED THU FRI SAT SUN

1. Draw an arrow to how you felt on the 'happiness' scale today?

2. These are 3 things I am grateful for...

1 _____

2 _____

3 _____

3. What did you enjoy most about today?.......

4. Who did you say 'thank you' to today?

MY 3 MINUTE GRATITUDE JOURNAL

DAY: MON TUES WED THU FRI SAT SUN

1. Gratitude

These are 2 things that really make me happy!

1. _____
2. _____

2. I felt happiest today when...

Write below what you did to be kind today?

_____
_____
_____

3. How I was feeling today...

Draw your face here.

MY 3 MINUTE GRATITUDE JOURNAL

DAY: MON TUES WED THU FRI SAT SUN

1. Circle where you felt on the 'happiness' scale today?

2. These are 3 things I am grateful for...

1 _____

2 _____

3 _____

3. What did you enjoy most about today?.......

4. Who did you say 'thank you' to today?

MY 3 MINUTE GRATITUDE JOURNAL

DAY: MON TUES WED THU FRI SAT SUN

1. Gratitude

These are 2 things that really make me happy!

1. _____
2. _____

2. Today is about expressing how you feel.

Draw or sketch anything you want below.

MY 3 MINUTE GRATITUDE JOURNAL

DAY: MON TUES WED THU FRI SAT SUN

1. I helped this person today.. ○○

2. Write below what you did to be kind......

{   }

3. Gratitude. These are 3 things I am grateful for...

1 _____
2 _____
3 _____

4. I would rate today....
Color in your 'STAR' rating for today.
1 star = I didn't have a good day
5 stars = EXCELLENT!

☆ ☆ ☆ ☆ ☆

MY 3 MINUTE GRATITUDE JOURNAL

DAY: MON TUES WED THU FRI SAT SUN

1. Circle where you felt on the 'happiness' scale today?

2. These are 3 things I am grateful for...

1 _____

2 _____

3 _____

3. What did you enjoy most about today?.......

4. Who did you say 'thank you' to today?

MY 3 MINUTE GRATITUDE JOURNAL

DAY: MON TUES WED THU FRI SAT SUN

1. My Happiness Rating
Circle how you feel?

- Happy
- Just OK
- I feel a little sad today

2. I would like to say thank you for...

1 _____
2 _____
3 _____

3. This person was kind today.

4. What did you enjoy most about today?.......

_____

MY 3 MINUTE GRATITUDE JOURNAL

DAY: MON TUES WED THU FRI SAT SUN

1. Gratitude

These are 2 things that really make me happy!

1 _____

2 _____

2. I felt happiest today when...

Write below what you did to be kind today?

_____

_____

_____

3. How I was feeling today...
Draw your face here.

MY 3 MINUTE GRATITUDE JOURNAL

DAY: MON TUES WED THU FRI SAT SUN

1. Draw an arrow to how you felt on the 'happiness' scale today?

2. These are 3 things I am grateful for...
   1. _____
   2. _____
   3. _____

3. What did you enjoy most about today?.......

4. Who did you say 'thank you' to today?

MY 3 MINUTE GRATITUDE JOURNAL

DAY: MON TUES WED THU FRI SAT SUN

1. I helped this person today..
....

2. Write below what you did to be kind......

{   }

3. Gratitude. These are 3 things I am grateful for...

1 _____
2 _____
3 _____

4. I would rate today....
Color in your 'STAR' rating for today.
1 star = I didn't have a good day
5 stars = EXCELLENT!

MY 3 MINUTE GRATITUDE JOURNAL

DAY: MON TUES WED THU FRI SAT SUN

1. My Happiness Rating
Circle how you feel?

- Happy
- Just OK
- I feel a little sad today

2. I would like to say thank you for...

1 _____
2 _____
3 _____

3. This person was kind today.

4. What did you enjoy most about today?.......

_____

MY 3 MINUTE GRATITUDE JOURNAL

DAY: MON TUES WED THU FRI SAT SUN

1. Circle where you felt on the 'happiness' scale today?

2. These are 3 things I am grateful for...

1 _____

2 _____

3 _____

3. What did you enjoy most about today?.......

4. Who did you say 'thank you' to today?

MY 3 MINUTE GRATITUDE JOURNAL

DAY: MON TUES WED THU FRI SAT SUN

1. My Happiness Rating
Circle how you feel?

- Happy
- Just OK
- I feel a little sad today

2. I would like to say thank you for...

1 _____
2 _____
3 _____

3. This person was kind today.

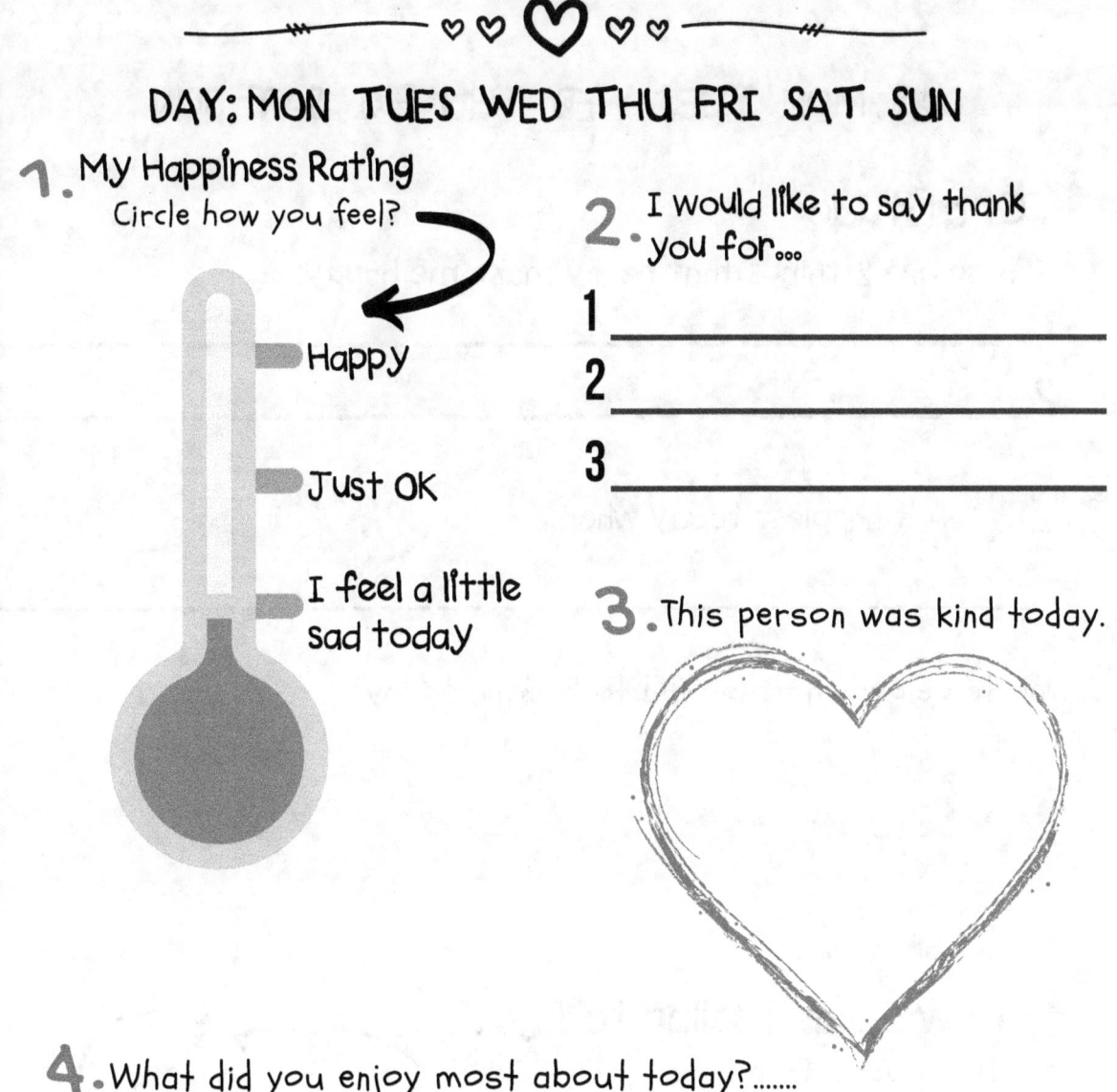

4. What did you enjoy most about today?........

_____

MY 3 MINUTE GRATITUDE JOURNAL

DAY: MON TUES WED THU FRI SAT SUN

1. Gratitude

These are 2 things that really make me happy!

1 _____

2 _____

2. I felt happiest today when...

Write below what you did to be kind today?

_____

_____

_____

3. How I was feeling today...
  Draw your face here.

MY 3 MINUTE GRATITUDE JOURNAL

DAY: MON   TUES   WED   THU   FRI   SAT   SUN

1. Gratitude

These are 2 things that really make me happy!

1. _____

2. _____

2. Today is about expressing how you feel.

Draw or sketch anything you want below.

MY 3 MINUTE GRATITUDE JOURNAL

DAY: MON TUES WED THU FRI SAT SUN

1. I helped this person today..
ooooooooooooooooooooooooooooooooooooooooooooooo

2. Write below what you did to be kind.....

{ }

3. Gratitude. These are 3 things I am grateful for...

1 _____
2 _____
3 _____

4. I would rate today.....
Color in your 'STAR' rating for today.
1 star = I didn't have a good day
5 stars = EXCELLENT!

MY 3 MINUTE GRATITUDE JOURNAL

DAY: MON TUES WED THU FRI SAT SUN

1. Circle where you felt on the 'happiness' scale today?

2. These are 3 things I am grateful for...

1 _____

2 _____

3 _____

3. What did you enjoy most about today?.......

4. Who did you say 'thank you' to today?

MY 3 MINUTE GRATITUDE JOURNAL

DAY: MON TUES WED THU FRI SAT SUN

1. My Happiness Rating
Circle how you feel?

- Happy
- Just OK
- I feel a little sad today

2. I would like to say thank you for...

1 _____
2 _____
3 _____

3. This person was kind today.

4. What did you enjoy most about today?.......

_____

MY 3 MINUTE GRATITUDE JOURNAL

DAY: MON TUES WED THU FRI SAT SUN

1. Draw an arrow to how you felt on the 'happiness' scale today?

2. These are 3 things I am grateful for...

1 _____

2 _____

3 _____

3. What did you enjoy most about today?.......

4. Who did you say 'thank you' to today?

MY 3 MINUTE GRATITUDE JOURNAL

DAY: MON TUES WED THU FRI SAT SUN

1. Gratitude

These are 2 things that really make me happy!

1. _____
2. _____

2. I felt happiest today when...

Write below what you did to be kind today?

_____
_____
_____

3. How I was feeling today...
    Draw your face here.

MY 3 MINUTE GRATITUDE JOURNAL

MEMORIES AND HAPPY MOMENTS

Do you have a photo that you would like to include here?

MY 3 MINUTE GRATITUDE JOURNAL

DAY: MON TUES WED THU FRI SAT SUN

1. I helped this person today..

2. Write below what you did to be kind.....

3. Gratitude. These are 3 things I am grateful for...

1 _____
2 _____
3 _____

4. I would rate today....
Color in your 'STAR' rating for today.
1 star = I didn't have a good day
5 stars = EXCELLENT!

MY 3 MINUTE GRATITUDE JOURNAL

DAY: MON TUES WED THU FRI SAT SUN

1. Circle where you felt on the 'happiness' scale today?

2. These are 3 things I am grateful for...

1 _____

2 _____

3 _____

3. What did you enjoy most about today?.......

4. Who did you say 'thank you' to today?

MY 3 MINUTE GRATITUDE JOURNAL

DAY: MON TUES WED THU FRI SAT SUN

1. My Happiness Rating
Circle how you feel?

- Happy
- Just OK
- I feel a little sad today

2. I would like to say thank you for...

1 _____
2 _____
3 _____

3. This person was kind today.

4. What did you enjoy most about today?.......

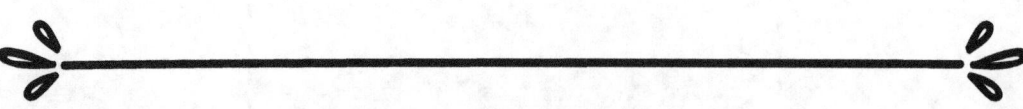

MY 3 MINUTE GRATITUDE JOURNAL

DAY: MON TUES WED THU FRI SAT SUN

1. Draw an arrow to how you felt on the 'happiness' scale today?

2. These are 3 things I am grateful for...
   1. _____
   2. _____
   3. _____

3. What did you enjoy most about today?.......

4. Who did you say 'thank you' to today?

MY 3 MINUTE GRATITUDE JOURNAL

DAY: MON TUES WED THU FRI SAT SUN

1. Gratitude

These are 2 things that really make me happy!

1. _____
2. _____

2. I felt happiest today when...

_____

Write below what you did to be kind today?

_____
_____
_____

3. How I was feeling today...

Draw your face here.

MY 3 MINUTE GRATITUDE JOURNAL

DAY: MON TUES WED THU FRI SAT SUN

1. Gratitude

These are 2 things that really make me happy!

1 _____

2 _____

2. Today is about expressing how you feel.

Draw or sketch anything you want below.

MY 3 MINUTE GRATITUDE JOURNAL

DAY: MON TUES WED THU FRI SAT SUN

1. I helped this person today..
_____

2. Write below what you did to be kind.....

{ }

3. Gratitude. These are 3 things I am grateful for...

1 _____
2 _____
3 _____

4. I would rate today....
Color in your 'STAR' rating for today.
1 star = I didn't have a good day
5 stars = EXCELLENT!

MY 3 MINUTE GRATITUDE JOURNAL

DAY: MON TUES WED THU FRI SAT SUN

1. Circle where you felt on the 'happiness' scale today?

2. These are 3 things I am grateful for...
   1. _____
   2. _____
   3. _____

3. What did you enjoy most about today?.......

4. Who did you say 'thank you' to today?

MY 3 MINUTE GRATITUDE JOURNAL

DAY: MON TUES WED THU FRI SAT SUN

1. My Happiness Rating
Circle how you feel?

- Happy
- Just OK
- I feel a little sad today

2. I would like to say thank you for...

1 _____
2 _____
3 _____

3. This person was kind today.

4. What did you enjoy most about today?.......

_____

MY 3 MINUTE GRATITUDE JOURNAL

DAY: MON TUES WED THU FRI SAT SUN

1. Gratitude

These are 2 things that really make me happy!

1. _____
2. _____

2. I felt happiest today when...

Write below what you did to be kind today?

_____
_____
_____

3. How I was feeling today...
    Draw your face here.

MY 3 MINUTE GRATITUDE JOURNAL

DAY: MON TUES WED THU FRI SAT SUN

1. Draw an arrow to how you felt on the 'happiness' scale today?

2. These are 3 things I am grateful for...

1 _____

2 _____

3 _____

3. What did you enjoy most about today?........

4. Who did you say 'thank you' to today?

MY 3 MINUTE GRATITUDE JOURNAL

MEMORIES AND HAPPY MOMENTS

Do you have a photo that you would like to include here?

MY 3 MINUTE GRATITUDE JOURNAL

DAY: MON TUES WED THU FRI SAT SUN

1. I helped this person today..
°°

2. Write below what you did to be kind......

{   }

3. Gratitude. These are 3 things I am grateful for...

1 _____
2 _____
3 _____

4. I would rate today....
Color in your 'STAR' rating for today.
1 star = I didn't have a good day
5 stars = EXCELLENT!

☆ ☆ ☆ ☆ ☆

MY 3 MINUTE GRATITUDE JOURNAL

DAY: MON TUES WED THU FRI SAT SUN

1. Circle where you felt on the 'happiness' scale today?

2. These are 3 things I am grateful for...

1 _____

2 _____

3 _____

3. What did you enjoy most about today?.......

4. Who did you say 'thank you' to today?

MY 3 MINUTE GRATITUDE JOURNAL

DAY: MON TUES WED THU FRI SAT SUN

1. My Happiness Rating
Circle how you feel?

- Happy
- Just OK
- I feel a little sad today

2. I would like to say thank you for...

1 _____
2 _____
3 _____

3. This person was kind today.

4. What did you enjoy most about today?.......

 _____

MY 3 MINUTE GRATITUDE JOURNAL

DAY: MON TUES WED THU FRI SAT SUN

1. Gratitude
These are 2 things that really make me happy!

1. _____
2. _____

2. I felt happiest today when...

Write below what you did to be kind today?

_____
_____
_____

3. How I was feeling today...
Draw your face here.

MY 3 MINUTE GRATITUDE JOURNAL

DAY: MON TUES WED THU FRI SAT SUN

1. Gratitude

These are 2 things that really make me happy!

1. _____
2. _____

2. Today is about expressing how you feel.

Draw or sketch anything you want below.

MY 3 MINUTE GRATITUDE JOURNAL

DAY: MON TUES WED THU FRI SAT SUN

1. I helped this person today..
ooooooooooooooooooooooooooooooooooooooooooooooooo

2. Write below what you did to be kind.....

{ }

3. Gratitude. These are 3 things I am grateful for...

1 _____
2 _____
3 _____

4. I would rate today....
Color in your 'STAR' rating for today.
1 star = I didn't have a good day
5 stars = EXCELLENT!

☆ ☆ ☆ ☆ ☆

MY 3 MINUTE GRATITUDE JOURNAL

DAY: MON TUES WED THU FRI SAT SUN

1. Circle where you felt on the 'happiness' scale today?

2. These are 3 things I am grateful for...

1 _____

2 _____

3 _____

3. What did you enjoy most about today?.......

4. Who did you say 'thank you' to today?

MY 3 MINUTE GRATITUDE JOURNAL

DAY: MON TUES WED THU FRI SAT SUN

1. My Happiness Rating
Circle how you feel?

- Happy
- Just OK
- I feel a little sad today

2. I would like to say thank you for...

1 _____
2 _____
3 _____

3. This person was kind today.

4. What did you enjoy most about today?.......

_____

MY 3 MINUTE GRATITUDE JOURNAL

DAY: MON TUES WED THU FRI SAT SUN

1. Draw an arrow to how you felt on the 'happiness' scale today?

2. These are 3 things I am grateful for...
   1 _____
   2 _____
   3 _____

3. What did you enjoy most about today?.......

4. Who did you say 'thank you' to today?

MY 3 MINUTE GRATITUDE JOURNAL

DAY: MON TUES WED THU FRI SAT SUN

1. Gratitude

These are 2 things that really make me happy!

1 _____

2 _____

2. I felt happiest today when...

_____

Write below what you did to be kind today?

_____
_____
_____

3. How I was feeling today...
   Draw your face here.

Color in the flower picture and relax today.

MY 3 MINUTE GRATITUDE JOURNAL

MEMORIES AND HAPPY MOMENTS

Do you have a photo that you would like to include here?

MY 3 MINUTE GRATITUDE JOURNAL

DAY: MON TUES WED THU FRI SAT SUN

1. I helped this person today.. ....

2. Write below what you did to be kind......

{   }

3. Gratitude. These are 3 things I am grateful for...

1 _____
2 _____
3 _____

4. I would rate today....
Color in your 'STAR' rating for today.
1 star = I didn't have a good day
5 stars = EXCELLENT!

MY 3 MINUTE GRATITUDE JOURNAL

DAY: MON TUES WED THU FRI SAT SUN

1. Circle where you felt on the 'happiness' scale today?

2. These are 3 things I am grateful for...

1 _____

2 _____

3 _____

3. What did you enjoy most about today?.......

4. Who did you say 'thank you' to today?

MY 3 MINUTE GRATITUDE JOURNAL

DAY: MON TUES WED THU FRI SAT SUN

1. My Happiness Rating
Circle how you feel?

- Happy
- Just OK
- I feel a little sad today

2. I would like to say thank you for...

1 _____
2 _____
3 _____

3. This person was kind today.

4. What did you enjoy most about today?.......

MY 3 MINUTE GRATITUDE JOURNAL

DAY: MON TUES WED THU FRI SAT SUN

1. Gratitude

These are 2 things that really make me happy!

1. _____
2. _____

2. I felt happiest today when...

Write below what you did to be kind today?

_____
_____
_____

3. How I was feeling today...
   Draw your face here.

MY 3 MINUTE GRATITUDE JOURNAL

DAY: MON TUES WED THU FRI SAT SUN

1. Draw an arrow to how you felt on the 'happiness' scale today?

2. These are 3 things I am grateful for...

1 _____

2 _____

3 _____

3. What did you enjoy most about today?.......

4. Who did you say 'thank you' to today?

MY 3 MINUTE GRATITUDE JOURNAL

DAY: MON TUES WED THU FRI SAT SUN

1. Gratitude

These are 2 things that really make me happy!

1. _____
2. _____

2. Today is about expressing how you feel.

Draw or sketch anything you want below.

MY 3 MINUTE GRATITUDE JOURNAL

DAY: MON TUES WED THU FRI SAT SUN

1. I helped this person today..
....

2. Write below what you did to be kind.....

{ }

3. Gratitude. These are 3 things I am grateful for...

1 _____
2 _____
3 _____

4. I would rate today....
Color in your 'STAR' rating for today.
1 star = I didn't have a good day
5 stars = EXCELLENT!

MY 3 MINUTE GRATITUDE JOURNAL

DAY: MON TUES WED THU FRI SAT SUN

1. Circle where you felt on the 'happiness' scale today?

2. These are 3 things I am grateful for...

1 _____

2 _____

3 _____

3. What did you enjoy most about today?.......

4. Who did you say 'thank you' to today?

MY 3 MINUTE GRATITUDE JOURNAL

DAY: MON TUES WED THU FRI SAT SUN

1. My Happiness Rating
Circle how you feel?

- Happy
- Just OK
- I feel a little sad today

2. I would like to say thank you for...

1. _____
2. _____
3. _____

3. This person was kind today.

4. What did you enjoy most about today? ....

_____

MY 3 MINUTE GRATITUDE JOURNAL

DAY: MON TUES WED THU FRI SAT SUN

1. Gratitude

These are 2 things that really make me happy!

1 _____
2 _____

2. I felt happiest today when...

_____

Write below what you did to be kind today?

_____
_____
_____

3. How I was feeling today...
Draw your face here.

MY 3 MINUTE GRATITUDE JOURNAL

MEMORIES AND HAPPY MOMENTS

Do you have a photo that you would like to include here?

MY 3 MINUTE GRATITUDE JOURNAL

DAY: MON TUES WED THU FRI SAT SUN

1. Draw an arrow to how you felt on the 'happiness' scale today?

2. These are 3 things I am grateful for...
   1 _____
   2 _____
   3 _____

3. What did you enjoy most about today?.......

4. Who did you say 'thank you' to today?

MY 3 MINUTE GRATITUDE JOURNAL

DAY: MON TUES WED THU FRI SAT SUN

1. I helped this person today..
○○○

2. Write below what you did to be kind......

3. Gratitude. These are 3 things I am grateful for...

1 _____
2 _____
3 _____

4. I would rate today....
Color in your 'STAR' rating for today.
1 star = I didn't have a good day
5 stars = EXCELLENT!

MY 3 MINUTE GRATITUDE JOURNAL

DAY: MON TUES WED THU FRI SAT SUN

1. Circle where you felt on the 'happiness' scale today?

2. These are 3 things I am grateful for...

1. _____

2. _____

3. _____

3. What did you enjoy most about today?.......

4. Who did you say 'thank you' to today?

MY 3 MINUTE GRATITUDE JOURNAL

DAY: MON TUES WED THU FRI SAT SUN

1. My Happiness Rating
Circle how you feel?

- Happy
- Just OK
- I feel a little sad today

2. I would like to say thank you for...

1 _____
2 _____
3 _____

3. This person was kind today.

4. What did you enjoy most about today?........

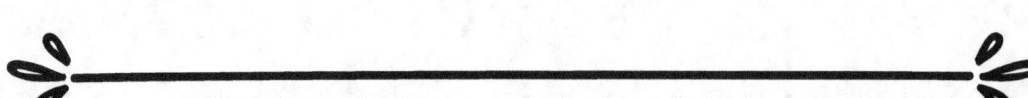

MY 3 MINUTE GRATITUDE JOURNAL

DAY: MON TUES WED THU FRI SAT SUN

1. Gratitude
These are 2 things that really make me happy!

1 _____

2 _____

2. I felt happiest today when...

_____

Write below what you did to be kind today?

_____

_____

_____

3. How I was feeling today...
Draw your face here.

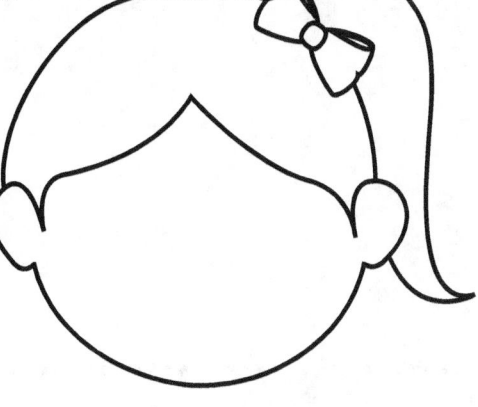

MY 3 MINUTE GRATITUDE JOURNAL

DAY: MON TUES WED THU FRI SAT SUN

1. Gratitude
These are 2 things that really make me happy!

1 _____

2 _____

2. Today is about expressing how you feel.

Draw or sketch anything you want below.

MY 3 MINUTE GRATITUDE JOURNAL

DAY: MON TUES WED THU FRI SAT SUN

1. I helped this person today..
ooooooooooooooooooooooooooooooooooooooooooooooooooo

2. Write below what you did to be kind......

{ }

3. Gratitude. These are 3 things I am grateful for...

1 _____
2 _____
3 _____

4. I would rate today....
Color in your 'STAR' rating for today.
I star = I didn't have a good day
5 stars = EXCELLENT!

☆ ☆ ☆ ☆ ☆

MY 3 MINUTE GRATITUDE JOURNAL

DAY: MON TUES WED THU FRI SAT SUN

1. Circle where you felt on the 'happiness' scale today?

2. These are 3 things I am grateful for...

1 _____

2 _____

3 _____

3. What did you enjoy most about today?.......

4. Who did you say 'thank you' to today?

MY 3 MINUTE GRATITUDE JOURNAL

DAY: MON TUES WED THU FRI SAT SUN

1. My Happiness Rating
Circle how you feel?

- Happy
- Just OK
- I feel a little sad today

2. I would like to say thank you for...

1 _____
2 _____
3 _____

3. This person was kind today.

4. What did you enjoy most about today?.......

_____

MY 3 MINUTE GRATITUDE JOURNAL

DAY: MON TUES WED THU FRI SAT SUN

1. Gratitude

These are 2 things that really make me happy!

1. _____
2. _____

2. I felt happiest today when...

_____

Write below what you did to be kind today?

_____

_____

_____

3. How I was feeling today...

Draw your face here.

MY 3 MINUTE GRATITUDE JOURNAL

MEMORIES AND HAPPY MOMENTS

Do you have a photo that you would like to include here?

MY 3 MINUTE GRATITUDE JOURNAL

DAY: MON TUES WED THU FRI SAT SUN

1. I helped this person today..
....

2. Write below what you did to be kind......

{
}

3. Gratitude. These are 3 things I am grateful for...

1 _____
2 _____
3 _____

4. I would rate today....
Color in your 'STAR' rating for today.
1 star = I didn't have a good day
5 stars = EXCELLENT!

MY 3 MINUTE GRATITUDE JOURNAL

DAY: MON TUES WED THU FRI SAT SUN

1. Circle where you felt on the 'happiness' scale today?

2. These are 3 things I am grateful for...

1 _____

2 _____

3 _____

3. What did you enjoy most about today?.......

4. Who did you say 'thank you' to today?

MY 3 MINUTE GRATITUDE JOURNAL

DAY: MON TUES WED THU FRI SAT SUN

1. My Happiness Rating
Circle how you feel?

- Happy
- Just OK
- I feel a little sad today

2. I would like to say thank you for...

1 _____
2 _____
3 _____

3. This person was kind today.

4. What did you enjoy most about today?.......

_____

MY 3 MINUTE GRATITUDE JOURNAL

DAY: MON TUES WED THU FRI SAT SUN

1. Gratitude

These are 2 things that really make me happy!

1 _____

2 _____

2. I felt happiest today when...

_____

Write below what you did to be kind today?

_____
_____
_____

3. How I was feeling today...
   Draw your face here.

MY 3 MINUTE GRATITUDE JOURNAL

DAY: MON TUES WED THU FRI SAT SUN

1. Gratitude

These are 2 things that really make me happy!

1 _____

2 _____

2. Today is about expressing how you feel.

Draw or sketch anything you want below.

MY 3 MINUTE GRATITUDE JOURNAL

DAY: MON TUES WED THU FRI SAT SUN

1. I helped this person today...

2. Write below what you did to be kind......

3. Gratitude. These are 3 things I am grateful for...

1 _____
2 _____
3 _____

4. I would rate today....
Color in your 'STAR' rating for today.
1 star = I didn't have a good day
5 stars = EXCELLENT!

☆ ☆ ☆ ☆

MY 3 MINUTE GRATITUDE JOURNAL

DAY: MON TUES WED THU FRI SAT SUN

1. Circle where you felt on the 'happiness' scale today?

2. These are 3 things I am grateful for...

1 _____

2 _____

3 _____

3. What did you enjoy most about today?.......

4. Who did you say 'thank you' to today?

MY 3 MINUTE GRATITUDE JOURNAL

DAY: MON TUES WED THU FRI SAT SUN

1. My Happiness Rating
Circle how you feel?

- Happy
- Just OK
- I feel a little sad today

2. I would like to say thank you for...

1 _____
2 _____
3 _____

3. This person was kind today.

4. What did you enjoy most about today?........

MY 3 MINUTE GRATITUDE JOURNAL

DAY: MON TUES WED THU FRI SAT SUN

1. Gratitude

These are 2 things that really make me happy!

1 _____
2 _____

2. I felt happiest today when...

_____

Write below what you did to be kind today?

_____
_____
_____

3. How I was feeling today...
Draw your face here.

MY 3 MINUTE GRATITUDE JOURNAL

MEMORIES AND HAPPY MOMENTS

Do you have a photo that you would like to include here?

MY 3 MINUTE GRATITUDE JOURNAL

AMAZING! You have completed your journal. CONGRATULATIONS!!

Be Creative!

Draw a picture or stick a photo here that was a special moment for you since starting your gratitude journal?

 # MY 3 MINUTE GRATITUDE JOURNAL

Journal Notes

Write here whatever you feel like. Is there something special you would like to include in your journal?

___
___
___
___
___
___
___
___
___
___
___
___

Other books by:

The Life Graduate
Publishing Group.

www.thelifegraduate.com/bookstore

www.ingramcontent.com/pod-product-compliance
Lightning Source LLC
LaVergne TN
LVHW060142080526
838202LV00049B/4055